PERSON OF INTEREST

BECOME THE PERSON OTHER PEOPLE WANT A PIECE OF AND CAN'T LIVE WITHOUT

MICHEAL J. BURT

Coach Burt with his greatest leadership influence,
Dr. Stephen Covey, a person of interest who impacted
millions of people around the world with his work.

ISBN: 978-0-692-75410-8
Layout and design by Sherry Wiser George
Editorial assistance by Mitzi T. Brandon
First printing: December 2012
Revised and updated: July 2016
Published in the United States of America by
Maximum Success, the publishing division of CoachBurt.com

Acknowledgements

The genesis of this book idea came to me while in The Strategic Coach™ program created by Dan Sullivan. Dan's lifetime of work with entrepreneurs, his thought process and pure genius, and his structures encourage people to multiply their future ten times and helped me accelerate my young entrepreneurial career so that I could attract other people to me.

To Dan Sullivan, thank you for helping this former basketball coach make the important transition to an entrepreneur who takes lower-level resources to higher levels of productivity.

While writing this book on a Florida beach, my greatest leadership influence and mentor Dr. Stephen Covey died as a result of a bike riding accident. He was 79 years old. Along with millions of other people, he deeply impacted my life from his teachings, his philosophy, and his third alternative thinking. The great basketball coach Don Meyer turned me on to his work when I was 18 years old, and it significantly changed my life forever. When Bill Clinton met John F. Kennedy as a young boy he was transformed and knew at that very moment he wanted to grow up and be like him. When I met Dr. Covey in Boston, Mass., at the age of 25 I said the same thing. "Maybe, just maybe, one day I can impact people like he did."

Rest in Peace, Dr. Covey. You will forever hold a place in my heart.

We all have a desire to be known, for success not to be too hard, and to attract people to us and our ideas. Marcus Ryan once said that the quality of our lives could be summed up in three ways:

How well we uniquely know ourselves,
How well we uniquely know others,
And how well others uniquely know us.

Many in sales have come to the conclusion that it's not how many people they know but rather how many people know them.

This book helps people know you in a new and different way. It will help you package and sell the special so that others are attracted to the incredible insight, energy, and ideas that you possess and share with the world.

Table of Contents

Introduction

If you asked, "How do I grow my business this year, make my dreams happen, or break through to the next level in life?" I would say you need to do two things:

1. Become a *Person of Interest that Is positioned properly to attract massive amounts of opportunity to you vs. having to chase it*

2. Build engaged followers by creating an experience that compels others to refer, discuss, and remark on

Both of these are not easy to do and could take years and are precisely why you need this book and need to get started immediately. If you want a brand lift, your phone ringing, and increased opportunities in all directions then you need to have the goods. You need to find Interesting problems that your unique talents can solve in proprietary ways that cannot be replicated or copied. You cannot give away what you don't possess and in today's oversaturated and over stimulated world people can pick up pretty fast if you're saying the same thing everybody else is saying and offering the same thing everybody else is offering. Many people are choosing price over experience today because we are not differentiating ourselves and clearly separating ourselves from others with our ideas, packaging, or marketing.

I have identified seven core areas that every *Person of Interest* must have. You may or may not have some of these but they can be acquired if you are willing to see the importance of building them into your life. Every major player in any industry most likely has these seven things. Some may overshadow others and compensate, but for the most part, they are consistent across the board and are the very reason these people are major players and not stuck in the minors. This is the special sauce. Once you have it people will want to know where they can find it and you'll begin to go places you only imagined. Most good chefs tell us that a dish that is missing a key ingredient flounders. So, too is a person that has "some" of the ingredients of a Person of Interest but not all. Yes, we can compensate in areas but when we have all seven ingredients and the free prize we begin to attract people to us like you can't imagine. We will be "on the inside" of where deals will be happening and we will become known, recognized, famous, and even celebrated in circles of influence.

This book came as a result of an encounter I had with a man named Dan Sullivan, founder of The Strategic Coach Program®. This is an entrepreneurial coaching program that top movers and shakers attend on a quarterly basis to gain systems and structures to elevate their lives. A participant only gets coached by Sullivan himself when he commits to $20,000 per year. Those that want to pay a lesser fee get coaches who have been trained by Sullivan but don't get him. In my first year in his program in session three of four Sullivan himself walked into one of my coaching classes, and everyone was interested in what he had to say. After all he was running a $20 million dollar company while simultaneously taking 155 free days off per year. In essence on his free days he doesn't do anything associated with work or anything that will cause him to think of his work. While he sat and shared with the class I feverishly wrote down page after page of notes, going fast because I didn't want to miss one word he said. I was curious on what ingredients he possessed that were so strong that people from all over the world would pay thousands of dollars to be coached by him, only to get one of his coaches. When he was finished I wrote down three words: *Person of Interest.*

Every person in that program wanted a piece of what he had. They wanted the freedom. They wanted the money. They wanted the expertise. And more than anything they wanted the peace of mind. He had all of those things and more. That's why I was in the class and would make the trek from Nashville to Chicago once a quarter year after year.

Months went by and I was speaking and coaching hundreds of real estate agents and lots of people in sales. They all wanted to know how to increase their markets and sell more, and I kept coming back to the same thing. *Selling is about attracting, it's not about chasing.* Oddly enough when I became an entrepreneur that was the lousy advice I had gotten from every successful person I met and spent time with. It looked like this, call 100 people per week, pass out business cards to everyone you meet, chase leads until them commit, and spend your time shoving what you have down other people's throats whether they want it or not. I have come to believe the exact opposite after running my expanding business for the past seven years and the reason for writing tis book. Selling is about having something so valuable that makes other people want a piece of you and it. It is about being perceived as the expert by what you project to the world in your brand, delivery, and follow up. When you have something they want you no longer chase sales. They come to you. People want to buy you a cup of coffee, pick your brain, spend 30 minutes with you on a webinar, and hear what you have to say. You have the supply and the market has the demand. You get to pick and choose who you work with, what you charge, and when you work. You are in demand and have so much demand you have to hire a team of people to handle your schedule, protect your time and energy, and help you sort through the right clients and relationships for you.

It's time you stopped chasing people and trying to sell them something they don't want and started becoming the something they can't live without. It's time you developed these seven ingredients that will have you so booked up you'll need a staff to manage your schedule. Today we start building the platform you've been looking for. Today we start the journey of building you into a *Person of Interest* and People of Interest build "Organizations of Interest." Today, I teach you how to build engaged followers who promote you and your brand on a consistent basis. Today, we start realizing your potential by pulling the goods out of you and packaging them in way that others say, "I want to have a relationship with that person." They are a "must have" vs. a "nice to have."

Let the journey begin.

Micheal J. Burt
Cabo San Lucas, Mexico
September 2015

The realization

I don't want to chase, I want to attract
"To attract other people we must become attractive." *Jim Rohn*

Any way you look at it chasing anything just sucks. You wake up and hunt something that usually runs as fast as it can away from you. This is the traditional sales approach. We're taught to chase leads, make 100 calls per day, follow up 7-15 times to close a deal, and hunt or bag elephants. My first year in business I lost $30,000. How did this happen? I woke up, had no idea how to attract people to me, didn't know or own a position in the market, fished in the wrong ponds, met and spent time with all the wrong people, and went virtually nowhere until one day I attracted the right person to me, and I didn't even know I was doing it. I wish someone would have come along and said to me the great Jim Rohn quote, "If you want to attract new business you must become more attractive." Thank goodness that person walked into my life.

I gave a presentation in West Tennessee for a bank that regularly had town hall meetings. The COO named Wib Evans was there and when I was done he walked up to me and said, "If you ever want a job in the banking business you call me because we will have one waiting on you." I attracted him with energy, packaged passion, a good message, and a lot of drive. That would eventually lead to a relationship that is still going strong and is based on these criteria which has come to be known as an "opportunity filter."

He is an *enlightened person*. He recognizes the highest qualities in others, sees potential where others see nothing, and knows he wants to play at a different level in life and is humble enough to know he has to have the help of others to get there.

He has a *unique perspective*. Based on years of experience, unique mentoring, and lots of success he has cultivated an interesting viewpoint in which others see value. This is valuable because I learn from him like he learns from me.

We share a *vested partnership*. We are in this together and have each other's back. There is no room for pandering, back room deals, or dishonesty. There is deep value in both directions. This is the exact kind of relationship you want with your clients.

This leads to a *collective passion*. We're all in on the relationship. We bring our A game to the table. We want to do BIG things together, not individually or separately.

This is what I call an *ideal relationship* and the ones you are trying to attract into your life.

The opposite of this happens when you chase clients, people, or relationships that do not fit in the filter. You end up with

- **unenlightened people.** They don't get it and you spend all of your time trying to convince them they can play at a new level or benefit from your product or service.
- **a common perspective** that you could get anywhere, that is boring as hell, and completely time and energy draining.
- **a one-sided relationship.** You do all the work and no one appreciates it. Nothing is ever good enough, and you'll end up trying to explain your decisions and going back and forth over trivial matters.
- **resentment and discouragement, not collective passion.** You want to strangle the other person quickly after the relationship begins and throughout the relationship. You

know deep down this is not a fit but you try every way in the world to make it work.

Now which one would you like to have? You could rate each of your relationships right now through this filter and decide which ones fit and which ones do not. The goal is to attract the ones that fit but we can't do that until we know what it looks like. I learned the hard way and am writing this book so you don't have to.

The great philosopher Jim Rohn (no that's not Rome Burning) said this,

"To attract other people we must become attractive." We attract others by our

- energy
- outlook and perspective
- knowledge
- appearance
- attitude
- packaging
- mindset and bigger future
- response to challenge and adversity.

The opposite of interesting is disinteresting. We become boring, saturated, or commoditized when we are just like everyone else, have the herd mentality, or have no real differential advantage whatsoever. So here is the million dollar question, "How attractive are you to the market in each of the areas listed above?" The great Dale Carnegie teaches us to "be interested" in others. This book teaches you to not only "be interested" in others but to actually "be interesting." People of Interest live fascinating lives, they associate with fascinating people, they travel to fascinating places, they achieve fascinating results, they cultivate fascinating impact, and best of all they are rewarded with fascinating money.

Get out of the mindset of chasing. It looks desperate and low budget and only happens when your sales are low, you can't create enough value in the market or your networks are too small. Quit being a hunter. Know this, you have something incredibly valuable that the world needs. You have unique talents, unique passions, unique abilities, and unique capacities. Draw people in and share it with them. Be uniquely you, and you will begin to attract the right people into your life who want to share in your gifts and talents. People of Interest are in serious demand due to the value creation they create. They don't have to chase, they are getting chased. They are the buyers vs. the sellers. They are the hunted vs. the ones doing the hunting.

{THE STORY BEHIND THE STORY}

In 2011 I was recommended to visit with a potential suspect (I never start with prospect because a person is not a prospect until they know who I am and how I can help them.) by one of my Target 25 advocates (these are 25 deep and meaningful relationships I foster as part of our selling system). "Great, my system is working I thought." I went and did a fairly poor job articulating my value to the entrepreneur and CEO of the company and didn't make any progress. I made a final plea, "Let me get in front of your sales team for 30 minutes at no cost to you." They agreed. I showed up, presented my talk on how to be mega sales producer in today's market and *they bought*. It seemed like a match made in heaven until we started the negotiating process where I would quickly find out the cost of not being a Person of Interest quite yet.

From that point forward it was a miserable game of lose-lose. The owner of the company beat us down on pricing (clue #1 they may not be a good fit), questioned everything we did even though it was clear his methodology wasn't working (clue #2), and vacillated back and forth between Dr. Jekyll and Mr. Hyde depending on which day you caught him (clue #3). The sales team was lazy and led by a person who protected them more than led them and the other leaders of the company stayed in a confused and fear stricken state because of Mr. Multiple Personalities (the owner of the company). At the sixth-month mark we had made little progress for all sorts of variables that I could not control. I knew the talk was coming of "Coach, you're system doesn't work." Well, no it doesn't work with the wrong players, lazy management, a fear stricken culture, and people who are not open to learning anything (usually some of the most successful egotistical ones). So what could we have done differently by not pursuing this partnership and how does Person of Interest play into this scenario that I'm sure many of you have faced multiple times in your life.

We should have listened to *our intuition*. Through multiple conversations in the negotiating process our gut was saying no but we still said yes, even at a highly discounted price from the beginning. You only do this when you are desperate and chasing vs. attracting. You are in a position of inferiority vs. superiority and this is a very weak negotiating position.

We should have created an *opportunity filter*® (Sullivan) to run potential opportunities through to see if they really fit with great criteria of the people we are looking to work with.

We should have been clearer from the beginning on *expectations*, variables that could affect the model, month-by-month plans, and our exact roles.

We should have had ***crucial conversations earlier*** with the client making him more aware of how his behavior sets people up to fail, creates confusion and chaos, and actually decays all the trust, not at the six-month mark when everybody, including me, was ready to jump off the building.

We should have ***pulled the plug*** at six months. Some people are just not worth the struggle. You're looking for people who value what you have to offer, not continuously question it. Some will see it and some won't, so what. When you get the vibe have the conversation and move on. Trust me, it won't cost you money it will free you up to attract more that is the right fit for you.

I mentioned the Opportunity Filter® Dan Sullivan created to ensure you are taking on great clients versus chasing bad ones. Every person should have a filter to run opportunities through prior to committing. Mine looks like this:

They have the *time, interest, and money* to be my client. I'm not looking for pretenders.

They are enlightened people. They want to play at a new level. I'm not trying to convince them that a coach can help them, they already know they need one because of their missing structures.

They have a unique perspective. I find them interesting and can learn from them, not boring and miserable.

We share a vested partnership. They don't blame me when they don't manage to do what I've taught. We are in this together and share responsibility together.

They fit in the financial parameters for my time, energy, and expertise. If they beat me up on pricing or consistently refer to it, I'm OUT with a capital O-U-T. They don't want people to beat them up on their pricing, so don't let them beat you up on yours.

Next we learn to make an important shift in our timing and get out of the sales business and into the transformation business. It will make all the difference in the world about how you see what you do and will pull people to you not repel them from you. To give away more we have to possess more. The key lesson of this chapter is simple, when you are not a Person of Interest you are in a weak selling position. Because of this you will take on any client that shows interest in you or your product. Like a lame guy sitting at the end of a bar just panning for attention from the female bartender you are at the mercy of others because of your value. People of Interest pick who they work with because of the market demand for them and their services. Sure they have to work a selling system and follow up in the "current of the urgent" world we live in but they are much more selective throughout the process and don't allow themselves to get into lose-lose relationships out of necessity. You may not be there today with your business but this is an aspiration to get to where we can always pick and choose who we work with and can turn down those that don't fit. You can only do this when our unique processes solve real problems for clients in interesting ways that they place a high priority on. Always remember this, "money only changes hands when problems are solved." People of Interest solve problems by marrying their unique skills and talents with needs the market has and they package up and sell those solutions in clear ways that the market understands.

Business of transformation

Stop commoditizing yourself.

People come to you one way and leave you another way. In essence people come to you confused, they lack clarity, and they are insecure about what their next moves should be. Because of the enormous skill set you possess they are changed. You have the knowledge, the skills, the desire, and the confidence to take those low thoughts of value and convert them to high thoughts of value.

They are transformed.

I listen to endless amounts of CDs, podcasts, and great intellectual capital. It sharpens my saw and gives me a competitive advantage in the market. In an interview I once heard Dan Sullivan say that everyone needs to be in the "transformation business." In essence, your clients, friends, colleagues, and family members many times operate from a place of insecurity and a lack of confidence and need direction in their lives in specific areas. Those areas could be personal growth, business, future planning, or money. When you become a *Person of Interest* many people begin to come to you from this place of weakness and because of your enormous confidence, knowledge, and skill set, you transform them. They seek you out, you distribute your goods in the form of a conversation, and they walk away confident and clear about their future and focused on what they can accomplish, not stuck in the pit they were in when they arrived at your doorstep. You're like a car wash that people go into in a dirty and unclear state and just a few seconds later come out clean and refreshed. You transform people from low levels of energy to high levels of energy.

Confused yet? You shouldn't be. Ask people what they do for a living. They'll give you the same old boring answers like real estate agent, banker, CPA, or insurance agent. How exciting is that? If you're like me you're already going blah, blah, blah. There is no differential advantage and nothing exciting about being a banker or motivational speaker or insurance agent. But when you make the transition in your mind to the transformation business, then you're changing people's lives, helping them play at new levels, becoming a game changer, and being a difference maker. This is a much bigger reason to wake up in the morning and a much bigger reason for people to sign up to be on your bus and on your team. I don't get out of bed to just grow a company five percent. Give me a break. I need something that excites my soul, revs up my engine, and makes me want to work up a good sweat so I know there's accomplishment.

When you're in the transformation business you consult, you coach, you change, you encourage, and you *blow people's minds*. **They come to you confused, they leave you on fire.** This is the transformation business. Sometimes I call it consultive selling. I wake up and coach the tee total hell out of people. I coach my staff, I coach my friends, I coach my clients, and I coach anybody who will listen. What do I coach them on? The business of transformation. Let's take low levels of energy and transform it into higher levels of energy through our knowledge, skills, desire, and confidence.

For this to happen you have to possess something that will help others get out of that rut. You have to have a unique perspective, a unique skill set, and a unique delivery. I believe there are five places to separate you from others. They include

1. **content**. Do you say common things in uncommon ways or have unique content that places you squarely in the interesting category?

2. **delivery**. The genius is in the sharing in a way that takes the complicated and makes it simple. Too many smart people are dumb at communicating. Success in one role doesn't justify failure in another. Get the intelligence of social skills genius or nobody cares.

3. **position**. Do you have a clear position in the market that you can own. This is not like all the banks that claim to be relationship bankers, or financial advisors that put you in charge of your own future.

4. **packaging**. This is simple. Is it clear to me why I should have a relationship with you? If not, you're too complicated. Hire someone professional to package your ideas in a clear and consistent manner.

5. **networks**. Do you spend time with those who multiply you? Best definition, again from Sullivan on referrals, "A referral is when great people tell other great people about how great you are." Refer-ability only happens when you deliver on the promise in such a way that compels others to talk and remark about how you influenced them in ways that others never could. You bring the "special sauce" to the equation that only you can based on your unique past, your unique mentors, your unique struggles, and your unique education.

These five things separate every great musical artist, every great business person, and every great innovator. Take them to heart and begin to diagnose where you have a "missing structure." With only a few of these things you'll fall squarely into a commodity trap of being good but with no clear differential advantage to compete on. Think of it this way, we must find out special, package our special, and then sell our special. Most have never found it and that's precisely why they are not People of Interest. People of Interest know their special. They know how to articulate it. They know how to share it. And their confidence grows and grows when they are playing in their special talent area. The world rewards this ability in the form of money, love, recognition, increased influence, and massive referrals.

I have a friend who is a real estate guru. When I need real estate advice that I'm confused about and need clarity I call him. He coaches, debates, consults, and offers his expertise so I can make an informed decision. When we're done I feel better. Just what the doctor ordered. A good dose of clarity which is what people are willing to pay lots of money for. How do people feel after they spend time with you? Are they more confused or more clear? If you take this "transformation" approach you are constantly looking for opportunities to share your wisdom and experiences with others in specific ways that takes those low thoughts of value and convert them to high thoughts of value. If you have ever been to a bad doctor vs. a good doctor you notice that they spend the same amount of time with you (5-15 minutes) but their knowledge transfer is so differentiated. With the good doctor you feel better about you when you are with them. With the bad doctor you leave still confused and lacking clarity. There is no transformation, only more confusion. If you can picture yourself as that "good doctor" that is always in the business of building up vs. tearing down then you are on your way to being a Person of Interest. You actually want thousands, if not millions of people coming to you for that transformation. The reality is that you can be a Person of Interest to just one person or one million people. This comes with an elevated status where people see you in an interesting way that owns the piece of real estate in their minds when they have a specific need that you can fulfill. Unlike any other you fulfill that need In ways that others simply cannot.

I have used this simple saying for years, "We cannot give away what we don't possess." If there's nothing in your tank how can you fill up other people with anything of substance? Go to work on you and your expertise so that when others call you have something to offer that is unique and different.

You're not just a banker, CPA, insurance agent, or motivational speaker. These are all commodities with millions of people competing for the same space. You're an entrepreneur with a very special skill set. You take lower level resources to higher levels of productivity. You take complicated matters and make them simple. You ease tense situations. You put pieces of the puzzle together faster or better than anyone else in the world. You break down ridiculous mathematical equations that people need in their lives into a single statement people can get.

Don't commoditize your own self by being like everyone else. I want to know why I should have a relationship with you versus the other 2,000 people who do what you do. I'm tired of seeing websites that start with the same template and do nothing more than cut and paste different pictures. Be different. Tell your story. Make it interesting. Be clear about what you really do. Give me a compelling reason to sign up to be on your team versus to have some boring relationship that loses my interest with the first pie chart and mission statement you share with me.

{THE STORY BEHIND THE STORY}

I coach "baby stars" into being "big stars." One of the bands I work with asked if they could use my tour bus to travel to BamaJam where they would share the stage with superstars like Eric Church and Tim McGraw later that evening. The trip started me thinking about how country superstar Eric Church has gone from a "baby star" to a "big star" in what seemed like a quick period of time. Something he does causes his following to *come alive* in a way that makes them want more of what he has. This endears him to his fans and attracts a huge following. This is exactly what you are trying to do, but you have to possess something they want for you to warrant their time, interest, attention, and ultimately their money. Getting and keeping people's attention in today's crazy busy world is getting harder and harder to do. This is where the concept of the *Big Five* came from I mentioned earlier in the book. From my perspective all People of Interest separate themselves by these five core areas. Their content is unique, their delivery is impeccable, their position is clear, their packaging is world class, and their networks are filled with nothing but multipliers (those who can expand their business in all directions.) The applicability of this for you is simple–focus on transforming ALL those that come to you by the goods that *you have*. Be a consultive seller who takes insecurity and turns into confidence. Turn obstacles into opportunities. Turn fears into solutions. When you're in the transformation business for lots of people, you become known as the go-to player in your industry.

Now we'll discuss how to make the major transition from a seller to a buyer. I believe a buyer always has a slight advantage over a seller any day of the week. The buyer is making the important decision to allot his time, energy, resources, and money to the seller. When we "flip this script" vs. the traditional sales approach of chasing and selling we are now "attracting" therefore becoming the "buyer vs the seller."

Buyer versus seller

The buyer always has an advantage over the seller,
so how can you become the buyer?

Flip this concept so that you are always the buyer who attracts versus chases. In any transaction the buyer always has an advantage over the seller because they are making the important decision to allocate time, energy, and resources to you and your product. With this mindset and this economy, people feel like they can negotiate any position they want and get you or the service at a cheaper price, placing you squarely in the commodity game, which is a game you don't want to play. This always puts the buyer at an advantage over the seller. You want to flip this script but can only do this when you're demand is so strong you are now picking and choosing who you work with, what you charge, and when you are available.

You become a *Person of Interest* because you have something incredibly valuable to offer the market. It could come in the form of specialized knowledge, skills, resources, or deliverables that you can drive like nobody else can. You become world class at this. When people begin to realize this by the big five I mentioned earlier in the book (content, delivery, position, packaging, and networks) they begin to come to you versus you going to them. When demand exceeds supply your prices go up and you start being selective about who you want to work with and how you want to distribute the talents you have, and in what settings. You can also raise prices based on the experience you offer the world, not an hourly rate, some convoluted pricing strategy, or other antiquated models out there. You have the goods. They want them and they will pay for them if it helps them drive some type of bigger future in their lives. Just as Tom Cruise can ask $20 million dollars to be the star of a movie, you will be able to ask higher fees because of some kind of results you can help them get that very few can offer the way you do. I've always said, "The bigger the problem you can solve the more money people are willing to pay for it."

You might be asking, "So how do I become the buyer versus the seller?" Great question. You can only do this when you hone your skills, delivery, presentation, and deliverables to the point that lots of people want them. In essence, you go to work on YOU not them. Too many people who chase believe it's as simple as a transaction. You have something of value to them (a product, service, or good) and people should just flock to you to get it. Problem is they also have 2,000 other people to buy it from. If they shop price they go the lowest route, and if you're more expensive you lose. This is why you have to find and articulate a differentiator, and that clearly becomes you. It occurred to me while speaking at a major event that you can win by having a differentiated product or service, a differentiated delivery of that product or service, or just by you cultivating such a unique perspective that you can literally achieve results that very few can in your field. You stand out. You look different. You run faster. Your skill set is just too strong to avoid.

Let's use real estate as an example as we coach thousands in this space. Go to the websites of the top five real estate agents in your market. Tell me what separates them from anybody else just listing houses or land? Very few of their sites tell us the one thing we really want to know which is "Why should I have a relationship with them and what makes them special?" You want to know based on their past results or methodology who can bring you the most joy to work with and get you the best deal. Websites that commoditize the agents simply have their picture, a small snapshot of who they are, and the deals. That's it. So let's just line up all 2,000 in the parking lot of the local Wal-Mart, blindfold ourselves, and pick one. It's like playing "pin the tail on the donkey."

The reality is that there are some who have more knowledge, more desire, more confidence, more likability, deeper networks, and better skills to offer. *Why don't they articulate that?* They simply go along and do what the industry says because that's what everybody does and the few who break the mode seem self-centered, egotistical, or self-promoters. Because of this scarcity mindset they go along vs. get better, they fit in vs. stand out, and they never create a separator. It's time agents begin sharing their "explanation of services" to others that looks like this:

1. Tell me what you believe vs. what you do
2. Tell me what you do as a result of this belief
3. Tell me how you do it differently than everybody else
4. Tell me all the people you have done it for
5. Ask me the big question, "If I could do the exact same thing for you that I've done for all these other people then what is stopping us from doing business with each other?"

This was taught to me by million dollar earner and top whole life producer Tom Love. He calls this the "Explanation of Services" and it's much more than a crappy elevator pitch. The elevator pitch never asks for business. It never articulates what your clear differential advantages are in the market, who have you have achieved fascinating results for in the past, what you believe and the real flaw it has is that it never asks you for the business. People of Interest know their "explanation of services." Because of the filter we mentioned earlier they know "who" they want to work with, "how" they can truly help them, and "what" it is that they really do.

You want potential clients to know one thing, "You only work with a certain kind of clientele." People who move from sellers, who seem desperate to buyers, who attract, make themselves and their businesses more attractive. So how do you do this?

. 1. **You meet the basics with appearance, presentation, and delivery.** They tell us that people make a decision if something is deletable in less than 2.7 seconds. Don't be deletable.

2. **You find small subtle ways to differentiate yourself from the competition.** I consistently use the fact that I'm a former championship coach vs. someone that just woke up one day and called myself a coach. I say, "Who is more qualified to coach you, someone who has actually WON a championship or someone who one day woke up and called themselves a coach. This differential advantage comes from your unique past, your unique education, your unique coaches and mentors, and your unique struggles. All of this must be packaged up in a way that the market understands and can appreciate it in clear and concise ways. (See *Go there in your mind*, page 23.)

3. **You study the market to the point that everybody knows you are the most qualified and can deliver the goods in a consistent and systematic manner to get them the results they really need.**

4. **You package yourself around your clear position in the market and share it as many ways as you can in clear**

and concise ways. The packaging must be shared in as many mediums as you can so you become better known, more famous in your space, and ultimately more celebrated by your clients that create massive referrals for you.

5. **You deliver on your promise.** You make yourself completely referable by practicing certain key habits that Dan Sullivan calls referability habits. They include

    a. *showing up on time.* He says if you show up 30 seconds late you decay fifty percent of trust with the other person.

    b. *doing what you said you were going to do.* Follow through which builds trust.

    c. *finishing what you started.* See ideas through to their logical conclusion.

    d. *saying please and thank you.*

All of these things make you and your business more attractive to the market. Stay away from being the class clown, the one upper, the contrarian, the constant Debbie downer, the emotional basket case, the relationship blowhard, and the consistent whiner about how life has treated you unfairly.

· *If it's not attractive to you, it's most likely not attractive to others.* What you want people to say is what one person said to me one time that was the best compliment I ever received, "I feel better about me when I spend time with you." Remember, we are trying to be both interested and interested. You are a Person of Interest when you raise the energy levels of the environments you enter, you make people feel confident, others don't feel judged in your presence, and you help people get off the fence on important decisions they've been wanting to make. In essence you bring a world of clarity to their decision making process.

They NEED you in their life. You are that "must have" vs. "nice to have." You dominate that piece of real estate in their mind when they make a buying decision around the services you offer.

Remember, people come to you confused and leave you on fire with clarity and purpose. This is always attractive to others. Become the buyer in the transaction versus the seller. Don't chase but rather attract because of the enormous amount of good will, content, and energy you put out. They will come to you when you expose more people to the solutions you can provide for them.

{THE STORY BEHIND THE STORY}

Becoming the buyer in any transaction begins by having the goods that other people want. This implies that you have to work on you to transform yourself first. Others begin to notice and start to want what you have in masses. Early in his career country music star Kenny Chesney came to Nashville and floundered for years. Although he had hits very few people in the industry took him seriously many times confusing him with Mark Chesnutt and calling him short, bald, and pudgy. Even while introducing him at the Grand Ole Opry they called him Larry Chesney. At that point he made a fundamental decision that he *would go to work on himself and start to change.* He began a rigorous workout schedule with a personal trainer, added an island flavor to his music, and started taking his career even more seriously than ever. The strategy worked making his music and appearance attractive to the market in masses. He would go on to put on one of the best live shows in the world and sell out football stadiums everywhere. It was his fundamental decision to go to work on himself that created this shift in his life and built his following of people. Now he's not the seller in any situation, he's the buyer. He gets to choose which venues he plays in, which products he endorses, which deals he closes, and who he wants to work with.

Oprah Winfrey said that one person cannot create a phenomenon. *They can only create something so profound and powerful that people's response to it creates the phenomenon.* What you create and who you are attracts people to you in small numbers or big numbers. Go to work on you so that you get to choose who you work with. You will become the buyer versus the seller in any transaction. When assessing how attractive you are to the market I like to look at what I refer to as your Person of Interest Assessment. It measures this:

1. Are you on track monthly and hitting your sales goals? (Yes or no)
2. Are you getting enough incoming demand for you and your product? (Yes or no)
3. How many people are calling your office or "seeking you out" to pick your brain weekly? (Notice this is incoming vs. outgoing)
4. How many strategies are you currently using to get your phone to ring as we speak to create qualified demand?
5. How many people are sitting in your "farm club" right now that are interested in doing business with you but have not committed to using your services (The Farm Club is a term that represents true prospects in my "Legacy Selling System" which is our top customer acquisition system).

Taking this assessment every 30 days tells if we are attractive or not. If we are not hitting our sales goals, do not have enough qualified leads, have no one calling our office for our time or energy, are using too few strategies to attract business, or only have a few people in our "farm club" then the market is telling us we are not People of Interest. When I was growing up in elementary school I remember a cheer our cheerleaders used to say that looked like this "U-G-L-Y you ain't got no alibi, you UGLY." I believe the market never lies. If you are not hitting any of your goals on the above assessment then the market is telling you that unfortunately right now you are ugly. The good news is that we can change it and become much more attractive by understanding the simple statement, "To attract other people we must become attractive."

Next we'll tackle how to find the free prize you have and how to package it and sell it to the world in a way the world gets and wants to buy from you and only you.

Unlock the free prize

Knowing, packaging, and protecting your special

I discuss free prize a lot when I speak and people always look at me confused and bewildered. Many years ago we bought Cracker Jacks for the prize inside, baseball trading cards for the bubble gum, and Lucky Charms for the gift. Each of these are free prizes, something unique and special that we got from purchasing that product or service. Each of us have a free prize that we can offer other people that completely differentiates us from our competitors. Seth Godin even wrote a great book on the concept called "Free Prize Inside" to speak to that something "extra" you get when you get that product. Our free prize comes from one place, our *unique past experiences* or *our unique and proprietary process* that cannot be copied or replicated. In essence this is exactly what other people are paying for. They are paying for our past education, our past struggles, our past experiences, our past mentors, our past breakthroughs, and our past learnings. These things help us create an experience that others can't replicate. They can replicate the product but they can't replicate the experience. ***Our past holds the keys to their futures.*** Now I know you're confused as we are taught our whole lives to *never look back.*

People pay me today to take complicated growth and make it simple, lead teams and people toward some dominant focus, package and deliver content to them in a way that helps them come alive, and look at other people's successful ideas and bring them to their equation. Where did I get these capabilities? **From**

one place, my past. Over the past fifteen years I've studied, thought, learned, gone to classes, watched gurus, practiced, and studied some more so that I can help people drive a bigger future. You have too.

Too many people allow their past to hold their future hostage. They think that somehow their past shackles them and doesn't benefit them. Nothing could be further from the truth. Your past makes you unique. Your past is incredibly valuable. Your past is where all the goods come from. If you accumulate key skills daily people will pay you for them at some point in their future. Think of it this way:

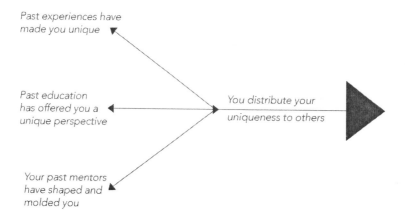

Past experiences have made you unique

Past education has offered you a unique perspective

Your past mentors have shaped and molded you

You distribute your uniqueness to others

I was raised by a young single mother. We didn't have much, but I watched her work and try to offer me a good life. It made me incredibly compassionate to others who don't have much and have to work for what they get. *This didn't prohibit me but actually propelled me.* I was raised in a small town with good people. It didn't limit my opportunities, it taught me how to connect with people of all walks of life and be good for all time zones. Perhaps you need to change the way you see your past.

We all have bad decisions, mis-steps, embarrassments, and dropped balls. This is what makes us human. We're imperfect people living in an imperfect world. If we leverage these unique experiences we can do better in the future. The past is finite. The future is infinite.

When you understand your past and what it offers you can now utilize it to help others drive their bigger future. Fill in the blanks in your mind (I hate doing it literally):

1. I had a unique mentor named

_____

who taught me this

_____

_____.

2. I went through a unique heartbreak when this happened

_____

_____

and it taught me

_____

_____.

3. I have a unique education in this

_____

_____

and it prepared me to do

_____

_____.

4. I had some unique struggles in my past that dealt with this

_____

_____

which has helped me figure out this

_____

_____.

5. There have been three unique experiences that have awakened me to my true potential and they were:

1) _____

_____

_____

2) _____

_____

_____

3) _____

_____

_____

    When you add all of these unique past experiences up, it creates your *free prize*, that special something about you that makes you unique. This free prize makes you valuable to the world because nobody in the world has gone through exactly what you have, had the same mentors you have, or have experienced what you have. This is you and you now have something strong to offer to the world. The question becomes "How do you package and sell your free prize?"

    This is where what Sullivan calls your Unique Ability® comes in. You can't package and sell what you don't even know that you have. Think of Unique Ability® as some superior skill which was factory installed in you, that you love doing, and the world rewards in multiples. This ability and your past experiences accrue your free prize that you sell to the world. Sometimes I refer to these talents as your "birthday gifts." They were given to you at birth but unfortunately you've never opened them. They were hardwired into you by the manufacturer. They were "factory installed." Until you know your "birthday gifts" then you can't really become the Person of Interest you were intended to become because you don't know your special. You don't know what makes you unique. You don't know what your competitive intelligence or differentials are.

Many people refer to me as a "Super Coach." This is a cross between a former championship coach who has an entrepreneurial mind. This combines a coaching acumen with intensity and focus to drive people toward a dominant aspiration with an entrepreneurial and business mindset due to my education, experiences, and business pursuits. It's what makes me unique to the world. I didn't just wake up one day and call myself a coach. I've actually won a championship and driven major results in both athletics and business. This makes me unique when it comes to teams and their leaders trying to take complicated growth and make it simple, get everyone involved and engaged toward the big goal, and keeping people motivated. That came from one place, *my past*. People are actually paying you for your past. Your past helps them achieve their bigger futures. Your past packaged into something special solves their problems much different and better than anyone else.

This is why I positioned myself with the concept of "Everybody needs a Coach in Life," and we are in a "Coaching Revolution" that says

- *you are a coach.* You are coaching and mentoring others.
- *you are getting coached.* You are humble and teachable and want to play at new levels.
- *you don't want a coach.* You are stagnant and closed off.

This is my position and how I package it based on my unique past. I also use action statements like

- We take your people and get better results.
- We solve problems you know you need solving.
- We activate the latent and undeveloped talent in your organization

What I'm really doing is packaging and selling my unique abilities to the world and competing on experience versus commodity. I could just say I own a leadership consulting firm or I'm a motivational speaker. That places me competing with thousands of others in this category and the market has no idea what my free prize is.

You have a free prize. This could be a tangible or intangible that creates a clear differential advantage and makes you a Person of Interest to one person or one million people. *To give it away we first must know what it is.* Then we must package and compete on it. There is something about you that makes you special to the market. You can do something that nobody else can do. Find, compete on it, and own it.

{THE STORY BEHIND THE STORY}

My first introduction to the free prize concept came while meeting a top financial advisor. I arrived at his office eager to meet the person others had told me about. His office was classy and filled with accolades, pictures with him and famous people, and props that he would use during his presentation. As he begin to illustrate the pain, the problem, and the solutions of investing and why his strategy was best he pulled into his bag of tricks to teach and share. He taught in parables. He broke down the complicated and made it simple for me to grasp. He was trusting and kind, had read my book prior to our meeting, and made me feel like a million bucks. Half-way through the presentation he asked me would it be worth it for me to spend a half-day with John Maxwell's key guy and even meet and spend time with John. I said enthusiastically, "Absolutely!" He said let me make some phone calls and arrange for these things to take place as I think they could add tremendous value to your life. I was hooked.

You see some people today merely believe that good service should cure all problems and attract more people to them. Nothing could be further from the truth. This is just the cost of doing business. *The free prize is something extra.* It's a sweetner that adds something to the equation. In this case the free prize was the aura, the networks, the knowledge, and the tremendous added benefits to having a relationship with this person outside of the transaction.

Some examples of a free prize for you could be

- your deep networks you can introduce people to that will help them move their ball down the field.
- your past experiences which can help people work their way through their current situation.
- your personality that makes people feel a new way about themselves.
- your deep knowledge base that helps people break through their complexities of life and helps them solve their biggest challenges.

- your mindset and motivation that keeps people motivated and on fire for what they are doing.
- your compassion that puts you with people at the lowest times of their lives and helps them fight through the struggles.
- your unique perspective on situations that helps people transform low-level energy to higher levels of productivity.

You have a free prize. Once you find it, you now know what your differential advantage is that you can exploit and attract people to you and package up with your marketing and advertising.

In the next section I teach you how to really differentiate by becoming a *zebra or a cheetah*. One looks different and one runs faster, and that's what we are all trying to do in the business world. There has never been a better time to look different and run faster than today. Everyone looks exactly the same. Everybody's marketing looks exactly the same. Everybody's branding looks exactly the same. Everybody's customer experience looks exactly the same. It's time you look different and begin to stand out vs. fit in. People of Interest pull themselves away from the pack in everything they do. They are clearly different than everyone else. I want you to look at every aspect of your business and ask, "What makes us different?"

Look Different. Run Faster.
Be Agile.

The zebra and the cheetah

People of interest look different and run faster and
they always see opportunity where others see nothing.
Dennis Waitley, author of *The Psychology of Winning,* has said
"If you go there in your mind, you'll go there in your body." If
I've said this once I've said it a thousand times. The *Person of
Interest* understands this; every action we take is driven by our
thoughts, and every thought is driven by our understandings.
Until we go there in the minds we will never go there in our
bodies. This is why it is vitally important in the accumulation
of knowledge mindset that you feed your mind with lots of
valuable information so that you can share it with others and use
it to your advantage. In some cases you become an information
entrepreneur with a very special skill set in your given field.
People call you to take the complicated facets of your industry
and break it down so they can become clear about it and make
decisions from a standpoint of confidence, not confusion. You're
a must have versus a nice to have.

Enter the zebra and the cheetah. In the animal kingdom the
zebra looks different than all the other animals. It stands out
in its appearance. It's easily recognized. It Is differentiated. The
cheetah is faster and quicker than other animals In the animal
kingom. In business and in life you need to look different, run
faster, and be more agile. The real entrepreneur sees opportunity

where other people see nothing. They see possibility where others see complexity. How can you look different and run faster in your industry so that it becomes obvious why people should have a relationship with you versus your competitors?

Here are five ways to create some real separation between you and the pack so that you too can become the Zebra and the Cheetah:

1. *Never, and I mean never, go where the herd goes.* Broad and wide is the way of destruction. Go against the grain, swim upstream, and know that people will not like it. Some will buy, some won't buy, so what? This isn't a popularity contest for your competitors to like you. *Here's a tip, they won't like you when you're kicking their butts.* I seldom won coach of the year as voted by my peers when I won the conference multiple times. It wasn't a vote on who did the best job coaching, it was a popularity contest so the people who created the least resistance won. Get over this early and use it as a motivator. You are not competing against others but against your own standard and potential.

2. *Develop a point of view.* This is why people are really paying you. If your point of view is like everybody else's, then why do they need you? Covey once said, "If two opinions are the same then one is unnecessary." A point of view stems from your unique perspectives on life and comes from your past experiences, who has influenced you, and your overall philosophy. Early on in your career you will borrow somebody else's until you have your own. Someday when you become famous others will borrow yours.

3. *Differentiate yourself in virtually every aspect of your business.* Break it down and look for both small and big ways that makes you different and better than everybody else. When I

was a coach I wanted our locker room, our offices, our uniforms, and our thought processes to be different. At Christmas, other programs went 15 minutes down the road. We put our players on a plane and flew them to California and Arizona. We used this as important advantages over other people. I can't compete head to head with John Maxwell or Tony Robbins at what they do, so I have to carve out a niche that is unique to me and my past experiences. When others in your industry have more tradition, more money, and more notoriety than you, don't compete head to head. Find the places that you can own and stay there.

4. *Package the differences.* Once you pick a position pound that position into the market. You'll know you have a good one when other people say it back to you or tell others about it. I love it when people come up to me and say "Everybody needs a Coach in Life." **Bingo!** This position comes from playing in your strength zone. Hire someone to package your ideas, not some dreamer but a doer. You have the dreams, you need them to drive the idea into intellectual property and marketing that other people can get easily so they can clearly see how you can help them.

5. *Attack the market like a Cheetah.* Cheetahs have a close ratio of 60%. They wake up and go on attack. They are always on offense and never on defense. This is a mindset that speaks to a Person of Interest. They create. They punch. They are never counter punchers. They plan weekly and daily and go on offense vs. defense. They have a real plan to attract massive amounts of people and opportunity to them. This cheetah mindset is unusual. Most are passive waiting on things to come to them. They react vs. create. The Cheetah Person of Interest knows this,

"Nothing happens until somebody moves" and "An object at rest will stay at rest unless acted on by an outside force." They become the outside force.

In an overstimulated and oversaturated world know this, you don't get other people's attention by saying the same thing and being the same. You get the world's attention by being a zebra or a cheetah. In my early days in the south I was taught to fit in vs. stand out, to go where the herd goes, and to look like everybody else. Even my own mother said to me, "Son you be seen but don't you dare be heard." In essence she was saying "Don't stand out. Just fit in." Conformity gets you nowhere. People of Interest are so valuable to the world because they have something different and interesting to say. They are needed in a world of sameness. The Zebra in you is longing to stand out vs. fit in. The Cheetah in you Is longing to run fast and create opportunity vs wait on it to happen. The Person of Interest also understands this: the opposite of interesting Is dis-interesting or boring. We have to be interesting to attract. The brain loves new, novel, and different. It hates anything that it believes it's heard before.

{THE STORY BEHIND THE STORY}

One day a buddy said to me, "You know, a zebra is different than all the other animals in the animal kingdom and a cheetah is faster and quicker." Just as Tony Robbins took the concept of Neuro-Linguistic Programming (NLP) and built much of his philosophy I knew zebras and cheetahs would be a new way to re-visit the topic of differentiation. I began to teach on the subject and eventually built a unique growth model on the system and methodology I would use to grow companies by upwards of forty percent in a one-year cycle. That combined focus, a proven system, the right activity, increased accountability, and a holistic plan to tap into all parts of a person's nature. This model eventually became a book I would co-write called "Zebras and Cheetahs."

To be a zebra and a cheetah you have to understand how to differentiate yourself versus others which starts by knowing, protecting, and packaging your special talent. The tie-breakers you cultivate come from the space and perceived value you can create in the market by the Big Five mentioned earlier in the book. Some people do this through their marketing, some through their language, some through the experience, and some through their referral system. It's vitally important that you begin to find even the smallest places you can claim that makes you different and better than your competitors and even more important that you're not a secret agent when you find these. A secret agent is the next best thing that nobody knows about. What most people need is one thing: **exposure.** I believe obscurity is the biggest challenge any entrepreneur has. This is where you are incredibly good but not enough people know it.

Here are some clear strategies to get the exposure you need to get the word out that you have the goods:

Cultivate a Target 25 of relationships and stay at the top of these people's minds. These people are or will become advocates for you and multiply the message to their spheres of influence. See them as an extension of your sales force. Be there for them at the crossroads of their lives, emotionally touch them on a frequent basis, help them move their ball down the field weekly, and refer the heck out of them. These 25 people will bring you more deals and send you referrals. Having great content so that they clearly see you as the go-to in your industry is vital. If you fall out of favor with these people they simply move on to someone else who can do similar things as you.

Practice the Showcase Strategy. Get out and speak and visit with as many people as you can about your product or service. Expose the market to the special you have to offer by cultivating a clear message around your position. You will never see me speak where I don't say "Everybody needs a Coach in Life."

Make a habit of working a connector strategy where you spend time cultivating multiplier relationships. Go where the fish are biting and spend lots of time with talent as part of your weekly system. Multipliers are people who have enormous reach that can "amplify" and "multiply" your message. My strategy is to connect with two connector per week.

The zebra studies the market closely and puts out things that either counter what others are saying in the market or contrasts to it. They are not contrarians just for the sake of being contrarian. They have valuable things to say and push back on things that are status quo and shouldn't be happening. **The cheetah** simply takes others ideas and does them better because of their attention to detail, their niche thinking, and their brilliant marketing. You may have the best thing since sliced bread but if nobody knows about it you're just a secret agent.

The zebra and the cheetah have a third alternative mindset that is open to anything and closed off to nothing. Where others see doom and gloom they see possibility. The closed off mindset will get you nowhere, and these folks are always open minded.

I'm giving you permission to stand out vs. fit in, to look at all of your collateral and ask this question, "What makes me different than everyone else in my industry?" If I'm the same then WHY am I needed?

Next we take a trip to Margaritaville. We're not going for the food but rather for the experience. To become a *Person of Interest* we have to learn to build engaged followers who are buying what we're selling and that doesn't come from the product (the burgers) but rather from the environment and experience we create.

Building engaged followers

A trip to Margaritaville: Learning to blow people's minds

I t was February of 2012 and I went to Dallas, Texas, specifically to hear two people: Jeffrey Hayzlett and Randy Gage at a National Speaker's Association winter meeting. *I went as a fan and came home as an engaged follower.* There's a big difference of being a fan of someone's work and being willing to pull out the checkbook and buy their goods. What good is it to have 10,000 Twitter followers if only two read your info, buy what you are selling, or pay any attention to you at all? I would rather have 200 stark-raving, crazy lunatics who hinge on every word I say than people who somewhat like what I do and are lukewarm toward me and my products. Building engaged followers is an art and involves creating an experience that transforms people. In essence, they come one way and after hearing or seeing you they leave another way. For this to happen you have to blow their minds and shock their systems in a way that very few have been able to do in the past. Gone are the days where you just give good service and they run and tell everybody they know how good you are. Remember, "Refer-ability is when great people go tell other great people about how great you are." You don't want a bunch of lousy people telling other lousy people how great you are. This would only lead to unqualified referrals.

So what was it that Randy Gage and Jeffrey Hayzlett did in Dallas? First of all they didn't hold anything back. It had been a while since I heard someone who didn't care about being politically correct, playing by the rules, being boring and nice, and putting me to sleep. These guys brought the energy but more importantly, *they brought the content.* Remember the Big Five differentials? Number one is content. Each of these guys had unique content, and they delivered it in a unique way that caused something to stir inside of me. I came alive. It encouraged me to come out of my shell, ratchet up the intensity in my presentations, and quit playing it safe when I was on the platform. When something awakens something inside of you, you want some more of it. It causes you to dig down deep and shatters all your preconceived notions and say one thing to yourself, "I can do this better." It was two things that made them stand out; what they said and how they said it. I walked away as an engaged follower who was buying what they were selling.

Let's take a trip to Margaritaville, Jimmy Buffet's restaurant chain. If you say that you go to this restaurant because the food is delicious something may be wrong with you. *It's not about the food, it's about the experience.* Just like the Jimmy Buffet brand and his concerts, long-time followers and engaged people line up, buy the fins, drink the drinks, listen to his songs, and have a party. When he comes back into town the next year, they'll do it all over again. These people are parrot heads. They're drinking the Kool-Aid™, believing in the message, and spreading the love. This is precisely what engaged followers do. So how do you build these engaged followers. Think about Jimmy Buffet. It's about how he makes people feel. It's free spirited, it's fun, and it takes you to a place that says "It's all going to be okay." At his restaurant every hour on the hour the giant airplane in the middle drops down a huge margarita machine, smoke starts coming out of the ceiling, the music gets turned up loud, people start dancing, the video screens show Jimmy Buffet flying over some cool island, and the party is ON. It's an experience that makes you want to come back for more.

Think about what the experience with you looks like. Is it boring, automated, and scripted? People feel like they're just another number and a name with no story. This is all too common in the workplace today. Know this, although people's faces may never show it, everyone has a story. When your story is intertwined with theirs, you become part of the fabric of their lives. They feel comfortable with you because of how you make them feel. You transform them.

Here are five ways to blow people's minds which is where "engaged followers" come from:

1. **Create some unexpected moments** that totally leaving them saying, "Did that really just happen?" People look for reasons to be turned off versus turned on. Give them multiple reasons to be turned on by getting lost in their dreams.

2. **Understand that small considerate gestures personalize any experience and differentiate and you from others.** Everybody else pushes people through like it's a factory. Be the exception. Take the time, invest the energy, and be in it to win it.

3. **Know this, service doesn't end after the sale, it just begins.** If you do this right every customer should send you five more customers. In real estate one transaction done right should be worth 5.7 more transactions. In the furniture business the average person will spend $75,000 in his/her lifetime on furniture. How much of that do you want? **All of it!** Every day with your current customer is an interview for your future customers.

4. **Be consistent throughout.** Don't make customers guess on who they are getting. You don't go back to restaurants

where the food is average and you **never** tell other people about lukewarm experiences. Make it remarkable. Give them something to talk about.

5. **Add so much value that they see you as a must have versus a nice to have.** Every contract in America will come up for renewal at some point. Don't even let it be up for discussion. Have this mindset: *They can cut other things out of their budget but they're not cutting me.* People are constantly making a decision about how to allocate their resources and in scarcity minded societies, like the one we are in now, people pull the plug fast on things that are redundant, boring, or not of use. Stay in the flow of your customer's lives or they will move on to somebody else quickly.

There's only one way to build engaged followers. Create an experience and share content that makes people feel a certain way about themselves and their futures. Get their dormant forces and faculties to come alive as a result of an interaction with you. This can be in the form of face to face, in your store, by seeing you on stage, by word of mouth, by what you write and they read, or what they hear that piques their interest.

Remember the concept of being referable. Great people telling other great people extraordinary things about you. This never happens when you merely meet the expectation you promised on the front end. It only happens when you drastically exceed that promise.

{THE STORY BEHIND THE STORY}

I was with a client at Old Hickory Steakhouse at Gaylord Nashville. The client said we just have to have this one person who will blow our minds. His name was Amir. We called ahead and asked if he was working, and boy were we in for a treat. Amir had grace, a smile, and the service that made us think there was no one else in the restaurant. Now this is what you expect when you have a $150 meal. At the end of dinner I was contemplating some dessert but didn't know which one I would have. Around this time Amir came to the table with three different types of dessert that were on the house and he had taken the time to write in chocolate syrup our names across the plate that said "Thank you for coming." The dessert was the icing on the cake and an unexpected WOW. *I teach people now to create a minimum of four unexpected wows as part of their customer experience.* These are moments that make the other person know you are the real deal, helps them understand that you truly listen to their needs, and shows them clearly that you have their best interests at heart. These can't be faked. Blowing people's minds combines the free prize concept with your zebra and cheetah approach to stir souls and touch hearts. It compels people to have a relationship with you over other people because of the way you make them feel.

Remember this, people will many times forget what you said, but they will always remember how you made them feel. Get down deep and authentic, bring you're A game to blow their minds, and leave them wanting more. This will take effort, planning, and an abnormal response from you. To get a new result you need a new behavior. We can't get new results with others with old responses. Blowing another's mind in today's world is harder than you think and easier than you think. Customer service has become so poor that one "free prize" may do it but what if you added four unexpected and concentrated things they NEVER expected. At Jimmy Buffet's restaurants they really only offer a few with the music, smoke, and gigantic salt shaker coming out of the ceiling. Just think if the food was actually any good.

Now we wrap a bow around this concept with seven important skills and attributes you absolutely have to have to become a *Person of Interest*. Here's the good news, once you know what these are you can go to work on developing exactly what you need to make the transition. If you're practicing what's in this book then pretty soon you're phone is about start ringing so much you won't be able to get to all the calls. You will have to hire a staff to manage your schedule and start exploring how you can grow your business around the genius inside of you.

Person of Interest

Seven Ingredients you must possess

All *Persons of Interest* share seven important ingredients. Don't ask me how I came up with these seven attributes. For years I've coached people around Covey's *Whole Person Theory* of body, mind, heart, and spirit. Each of these parts produces four different intelligences, four different dimensions, and four different manifestations. The body represents physical intelligence and the discipline to act. It also represents skill. For the mind it represents knowledge or know how. For the heart it represents passion, compassion, and emotional intelligence—one of the most important intelligences to have. For the spirit it represents belief in self, in a higher power, and confidence to offer up one's best and highest self to the cause. This helps me to diagnose quickly where someone needs coaching but it also leads me to believe that if a person had all four of these—**knowledge, skills, desire, and confidence** that other people would be attracted to them. It would look like this:

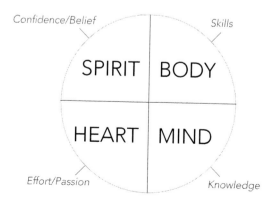

Think about the people you follow and are attracted to. They *have knowledge for the mind, skills for the body, effort for the heart, and confidence for the spirit. These are attractive qualities.* People with skills who are lazy, and who have knowledge without discipline, talent without effort, effort without talent, or confidence without skill, talent, or knowledge are simply not that attractive to the market. This model begins the process to knowing where you need to go to work on yourself so that you possess more so you can offer more to the world. Remember this, "People don't buy into the dream until they buy into the dreamer." We become more attractive to the market when we have more to offer masses of people, and we are the solutions to their challenges.

But then it hit me. This is an incomplete paradigm for a **Person of Interest.** I knew people that had these four things but were lacking in other areas and I knew exactly what those areas were. A person lacking all seven ingredients are lacking or fragmented as it relates to the Person of Interest paradigm. With all seven you're attractiveness goes through the roof. People will be knocking down your door to get to what you've got. The additional four ingredients to accompany knowledge, skills, desire, and confidence are:

- *likability.* The ability for others to genuinely like you. This is a deal breaker if you don't have it. Think of this as "energy" and energy cannot be created, only transferred.
- *connectivity.* The ability to be "good for all time zones" and connect with everyone instantly. Think of this was as easy to connect with, able to effectively communicate to varying kinds of people, and not intimidated when around people with superior skill sets.

• ***deep networks.*** The ability to have deep and wide networks of advocates that are actively promoting you and following your work.

• ***free prize.*** The ability to know what special you have to offer and package it up in a way that others easily understand why they should have a relationship with you. This is the "extra" or "sweetner" you or your company offer that are not part of the deal that others get "in addition" to what you promised.

These seven ingredients and the "free prize" complete the ***Person of Interest paradigm.*** What good would it do if you had knowledge, skills, effort, and confidence but a very low likability? Or what if you had all of the above but didn't know your free prize; therefore, you unintentionally commoditize yourself by practicing the herd mentality and doing what everybody else tells you to do? What if you have natural talent but no grind or effort so you just waste it? Not very attractive huh?

The key is to make a serious effort to go to work in each area. So here is how you can work in each area to become that person that other people can't live without.

KNOWLEDGE
{ *Spend lots of time with talent and don't talk, just listen.*
{ *Read everything you can get your hands on.*

SKILLS
{ *One word: Practice.*
{ *Ask for feedback on your delivery of your knowledge.*

EFFORT
{ *Will you pay the price or not?*
{ *Do the heavy lifting to get from point A to B.*

CONFIDENCE
{ *Get some mini-victories—Private victories precede public ones.*
{ *Don't ever give your confidence up to anyone else.*

LIKABILITY
- *Smile more and talk less.*
- *Don't be contrarian, one upper, or know it all.*

DEEP NETWORKS
- *Get lost in other people's dreams, period.*
- *Be a giver versus a taker in every transaction.*

CONNECTIVITY
- *Get over yourself. You can learn anything from anybody.*
- *People have a story; get to know it.*

FREE PRIZE
- *Package and sell your special.*
- *Know your true unique gifts and "protect the special."*

So that it is very clear, the *Person of Interest* has seven core ingredients and some free prize you are sharing with the world. It would look like this:

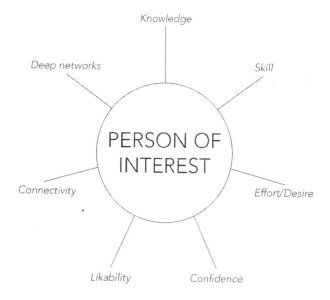

Your free prize could be a variation of all seven of these or that you have an incredible knowledge set or skill set in one specialized area that helps people in unique ways. If you are serious about being a *Person of Interest* then you will actively begin the process of growing and cultivating each of these seven things coupled with the key mindsets and ingredients of the book.

Think of it like this. People who attract other people have something incredibly valuable that other people want and will pay for. Now that you have a filter and lens to look through you can go to work on possessing more so that people will want more.

Now it's that time. It's time to go forth and conquer. You have the goods you need now to start building some stark-raving fanatics for YOU.

{THE STORY BEHIND THE STORY}

Wouldn't it be nice if you could wake up and have so much opportunity that you could pick and choose who you work with for what price? *People of interest have these options.* They don't chase, they attract and they attract for one reason, they're attractive. They put out certain skills and attributes that other people want. The first question for you is this: How attractive am I to the market? This may take the help of others so you can see if you have a perception problem or not. The key is creating work that is so compelling that the masses want what you have to offer. If you have this content then it's time to expose people to it. Remember, we can't be that secret weapon. Many of the greats we know like Jobs, Robbins, and others were brilliant marketers of their products. People buy into them and therefore buy into what they are selling. I started following Dan Sullivan because so many enlightened people were telling me about him and his program. This was the draw but when I began to discover his content it hooked me. He had the missing structure I was looking for and needed to grow my business.

People of interest understand that they are pulling people to them not pushing what they have on others. Like magnets people are drawn to their vision, their motivation, their skill sets, and their philosophy. Now that you have a clear structure to go and work on you can diagnose what areas you and your business need the most work and get to work. This book may make you rethink your strategies and re-work what you put out to the world.

You may have been thinking that this book has been about "self-promotion" of how to get your name out there and separate yourself by becoming a Person of Interest. At first when I wrote this it was. Over the last few years I've matured and come to understand that being a Person of Interest is not for you. It's not for you to become famous, well known, renowned, or even celebrated. It's actually for others. You see the real reason you should aspire to become a Person of Interest is for the impact and influence you can attain. The more people who know you and come to you because of what you have opens the door for you to impact the many. The higher your Person of Interest score is then the greater you can help others with your unique talents.

In 1996 Mother Teresa checked into a hospital in La Jolla, California. She had been In Tijuana just 20 miles across the border helping others when she contracted bacterial pneumonia. In most settings the people in hospitals with an elevated Person of Interest status is the physicians. In this case the script was flipped. The doctors clamored over who would serve her and be able to say, "I am Mother Teresa's physician." Their tactics and strategies didn't work on her. She told them that she may or may not take their advice but she did have a request. She began to ask physicians this question, "How many of you have gone across the border to Tijuana to help those in need but can't afford it?" The doctors said none. She said, "As long as I am In this hospital I will place a sign-up sheet" on the outside door for you to sign up to help the needy. One by one they signed up to go across the border to help with their services, for free. She used her Person of Interest score to do one thing, impact others and influence their decisions. At the end of the day this is the real reason you should aspire to become a Person of Interest. It's to take your unique and differentiated talents and distribute them to the world for greater and greater impact.

Every morning I affirm this in me. "I am a Person of Interest. Success is my duty, it's my obligation, and it's my responsibility. People are counting on me to show up and deliver the goods, not for me, but for them. When you attain the seven ingredients and the free prize we discuss in this book and go to work on possessing more so you can give away more the demand for you and your talents will become so strong that you will always be the buyer vs. the seller, just like Mother Teresa.

You are now ready to open your birthday gifts and share them with the world. God bless you. I can't wait to see the impact you are now going to have.

Afterword

Go Forth and Conquer

You are now ready to attract people to you. I remember an interesting show I used to watch on VH1 called "The Pick-Up Artist." A person named "Mystery" had perfected the art of picking women up at a bar and was so talented at it that he began to teach other people his systems and methodologies of attraction. He would take uninteresting guys and coach them through a process to elicit interest from others. He built their confidence, made them believe in their own selves, and gave them a plan. He made them more attractive to the market. You too can become more attractive to the market by focusing on the contents of this small but powerful book. I've studied some of the most talented people in the world and they have these characteristics. I'm not convinced it is purely nature and they were born that way. In lots of ways Steve Jobs was a rebel but could be incredibly likable when he wanted to. He became a *Person of Interest* to the world. You can too.

I believe you have the goods. You just need a filter, a plan, a coach, and a new structure to become a person that has so much to offer the world that people can't wait to buy it and will line up to get some of what you're offering. When you go to work on you so that you can possess more in each of these key areas and you adopt some of the guiding principles included, you will begin to stand out in a noisy and crowded world. Your phone will begin to ring. Your schedule will begin to be booked. You will have to look at how to scale your efforts because you won't be able to be in multiple places at one time. You will start looking at how to cultivate passive harvest income so you can make money when you're not there, and you will begin to build a regional, super-regional, national, and global brand. You will manifest such a bigger future that people will be asking you how you did it, and they'll even pay you to tell them.

As my coach once taught me, when you become a *Person of Interest* people will pay you just to show up. And then they will pay you again just to open your mouth.

Now go forth can conquer. Let the world know what you have to offer.

About the Author

Coach Micheal Burt is quickly becoming the *Person of Interest* he writes about in this book. A former championship women's basketball coach, Micheal quickly rose through the coaching ranks by infusing his coaching acumen with his entrepreneurial mindset and his incredible focus and intensity. He became known for his deep ability to move groups of people toward a dominant focus by being a leader people were attracted to. At 25 Micheal began writing his first of eleven books, speaking nationally, and helping companies drive dominant aspirations in sales, culture, and leadership. He is the founder of Micheal Burt Enterprises, LLC, and The Greatness Factory and has a clear position in the market that *Everybody needs a Coach in Life.* Go to www.coachburt.com to learn more.